Voices *for* Good Friday

Worship Services with Dramatic Monologues Based on the Gospels

Amanda J. Burr

Abingdon Press
Nashville

To my Uncle Phil, who was, after Mom and Dad, my first fan

Voices for Good Friday

Copyright © 2014 by Abingdon Press

ISBN 978-1-4267-8314-2

This book is printed on acid-free paper.

Scripture quotations are from the New Revised Standard Version of the Bible, copyright 1989, Division of Christian Education of the National Council of the Churches of Christ in the United States of America. Used by permission. All rights reserved.

Hymnal references in the worship services are *The United Methodist Hymnal*, copyright © 1989 by The United Methodist Publishing House; and *The Faith We Sing*, copyright © 2000 by Abingdon Press.

14 15 16 17 18 19 20 21 22 23—10 9 8 7 6 5 4 3 2 1
MANUFACTURED IN THE UNITED STATES OF AMERICA

Contents

Preface

Blame it on Frederick Buechner and his book *Telling the Truth: The Gospel as Trage-dy, Comedy, and Fairy Tale*. Following in the tradition of the *Haggadah Midrash,* so cherished in ancient Judaism, I have been writing stories based on Scripture for the past twenty-seven years. The people in Scripture are real with three-dimensional lives. These stories about them are like literary 3-D glasses designed to lift the characters up and out of the pages of the text.

The people chosen from the Gospel of Matthew are those on the margins, outsiders of the community of faith. They are people Jesus never touched, but whose lives he changed along the way.

Mark writes about the suddenness of God and uses action words to tell stories. The people in these stories encounter Jesus and are changed or healed quite suddenly.

The people chosen from the Gospel of Luke are those whose lives were changed as they reached out to care for Jesus. The central character of the Luke narratives is the perfumed oil named the Balm of Jericho.

Introduction

HOW TO USE THE STORIES

This book is divided by lectionary year, so the stories in each section correspond with stories from the gospel designated for that lectionary year:

Year A (Matthew)—On the Margins

Year B (Mark)—Out of Darkness

Year C (Luke)—There Is a Balm

I wrote these stories for Good Friday services in the congregations I have served, inviting church members to play the different characters. The stories are first-person accounts and should, therefore, be delivered as monologues or, in the case of the Gadarenes, as dialogue. The person or persons telling the story *are* the eyewitnesses. The story they are telling is their story.

Encourage readers to read *even more slowly* than they think is slow enough, so they don't stumble as they read. When a reader stumbles, it is because he or she is reading too fast. *Slow down.*

I remember having the opportunity to do what is called an "under-fives" (under five lines) on *Days of Our Lives* many years ago. Being trained as a stage actress, I naturally project my voice, but the TV folks kept telling me to tone it down: "You don't have to speak so loud." There was a boom microphone right over my head, and I guess my voice *projecting* was blowing out the eardrums of the sound technician.

A microphone does not make up for, or magically improve, inarticulate speech. So encourage the readers to **ar-tic-u-late** their words.

If any of the readers for the monologues have trouble with their eyesight and need really large print, give them a large-print script for easier reading.

Setting Your Stage

These stories have been used in an evening service, whether a service of darkness—Tenebrae—or the pastor's own format. With each set of stories, I have included worship service formats that you can use. There are a number of Tenebrae service formats that intermingle Scripture, hymns, and the gradual darkening of the sanctuary. These stories can be used in most service formats as the homiletic portion of the service—one after another or spread out.

As Reader's Theater

For a reader's theater format, do use handheld microphones. Readers can be seated on stools or chairs with microphones set on stands in front of them.

Have the readers dressed in black (no bling or spangles). When one reader is reading, the other readers are still. They should **not** be turning the pages of the script following along with the current reader. They should remain focused on their own script or the person reading. It is important that they remain still so as not to distract or detract from the telling of the story. The service is designed to flow by means of these stories.

As a Staged Performance

For a staged performance, actors should memorize their monologues. If they are not prepared to memorize the piece, then it is reader's theater and should be performed as instructed above.

As Pulpit Narration

In this setting, each actor steps into the pulpit or up to the lectern and delivers the monologue, in the same focused way used in the reader's theater setting. If you choose to use the worship formats included in this book where Scripture is intermingled in the liturgy, the dramatic reading following the Scripture or a hymn, I would advise utilizing both the lectern and the pulpit, alternating them to keep the service flowing.

On the Margins

NARRATIVES BASED ON THE GOSPEL OF MATTHEW

Characters for Readings

- The Gadarene Dmoniacs, Matthew 8:28-34
- The Canaanite Woman (Her Daughter Speaks), Matthew 15:21-28
- The Centurion, Matthew 8:5-13; 27:54

Intended Message of These Stories

The stories based on Matthew's Gospel are told through the eyes of people whose culture and background is different from that of Jesus'. They are outside the social, cultural, ethnic, and religious circles of Jesus. They are on the margins of his ministerial outreach—until they meet. These people found a way to connect with Jesus, or Jesus found a way to connect with them, in spite of the barriers between them.

THE GADARENE DEMONIACS
Matthew 8:28-34

Director's Note: The challenge of this story in Matthew's text is having *two* demoniacs living among the tombs out on the outskirts of Gadara. In Matthew's story Jesus has crossed to the eastern shore of the Sea of Galilee, entering the area known as the Decapolis. The ten cities that make up the Decapolis are centers of Greek and Roman culture.

I have made Matthew's Gadarene demoniacs brothers—twin brothers (they can be fraternal twins). Two readers will tell their story together. They have a sense of humor and tease each other, but are devoted. Surprisingly, they are not angry or resentful men. They are sensitive to each other's feelings about the course of their lives, before meeting Jesus and afterwards.

Adel (short for Adelphos, meaning "born of the same womb—brother") is only minutes older than Phee (short for Philon, meaning "to love"), but takes the role of older brother seriously. He sees himself as Phee's protector, usually trying to protect Phee from himself. Phee is daring, always pushing the limits of his body and his mind. These twins may live among civilized people now, but the reader might display a tentativeness in his speech, as language is still new to Adel and Phee.

The Gadarene Demoniacs

Adel: I'm Adel.

Phee: And I am Phee.

Adel: As far back as I can remember, it has always been Phee and me together. We are like two halves of the same person.

Phee: I am the better looking half.

Adel: That's right, but I'm older and wiser.

Phee: By a minute.

Adel: Before we were rescued, we were never apart. I remember the woman taking us from the dark room where we lived. It was dark outside too. She brought us to a faraway place of rocks and caves, and gave us a bag with food in it and left.

Phee: She never came back.

Adel: We were so afraid, we cried and held on to each other, trying to keep warm in the caves. We saw people, but hid from them because everyone who came to live in that place was dead. Everyone except us.

Phee: What Adel means is people brought the dead to this place. They left them there just like we were left. We took care of them and kept watch so they would be safe. We slept in the daytime, hiding ourselves in the tombs, and we kept our people company through the night.

Adel: At night we looked for food. There were fruit trees all around and water. When the swineherds on the hillside killed a pig to eat, we would sneak into their camp while they slept and take whatever they discarded. We gnawed on the pig bones until there was nothing left, inside or out.

Phee: As we survived and grew, we made tools from the bones, sharpening them into knives to cut branches from the trees. We cut linen from the shrouds covering our dead friends and wrapped ourselves in it to keep warm. We learned to make fires by watching the swineherds.

Adel: We were discovered one very cold night. While sneaking back to the tombs from the swineherds' camp, we stumbled over one of them in the bushes. He ran after us, but stopped at the edge of the graveyard. He would never have found us in the dark.

Phee: The next day the man who chased us came back with some other men. When they found us sleeping in one of the tombs, they dragged us out into the open, yelling and screaming at us. We didn't understand them. They sounded like the wild animals of the night, and we began to howl in response to their howling. They beat us and left us with our hands and feet bound by leather straps.

Adel: Phee was beaten so badly he was unconscious for a long time. I rolled over onto my knees and chewed the leather straps off his hands and feet. When he finally came to and was able to move, he cut off my bindings and we crawled back into the safety of the tombs.

Phee: There had always been a chance that we might be discovered, but until now we hadn't realized that discovery might cost us our lives. We had to figure out how to keep people away from us, away from the tombs. We had to frighten them away.

Adel: After that, when people came to bury their dead we growled and snarled from behind the rocks and shook the bushes. Most people ran away. When the swineherds came looking for us we were ready with slings and stones. We had excellent aim. Now we were older, bigger, and much stronger. If they came near we jumped down from the rocks and ran after them slinging stones at their heads and hind ends.

(**Note to the Readers:** *Pick up the pace in this section as the two of you complete each other's sentences and the dialogue gets more intense. Don't speed up, just make the way you say the words more intense. More angst is good, even a remembrance of the fear you felt that day, but DO NOT READ FASTER.)*

Phee: *No one came near the tombs anymore because we made it a fearful place. It was the only way we knew to be safe in our home...*

Adel: *...* until the day that Jesus, the Galilean, came and changed everything.

Phee: We were tending our gardens and pruning our fruit trees when we noticed him watching us. So we became fierce, stooping low and growling...

Adel: ...moving toward him with our hands raised, ready to lunge if he didn't run away.

Phee: We shouted and cried in our language: "What are you doing here? Go away! You have nothing to do with us."

Adel: He didn't move! He didn't blink an eye. I had never seen such a face. There was no fear in his face. His eyes weren't like the eyes of the people who brought their dead to the tombs.

Phee: His eyes weren't like the eyes of the swineherds who beat us.

Adel: The noises he made were strong noises, but they didn't sound sad or angry or mean. We didn't understand his sounds.

Phee*:* We had to protect each other and our home. We ran straight at him, screeching our loudest and most terrifying cries. We planned to knock him down and then let him scramble away.

Adel: But we didn't knock him down. We slammed into his body, full force—both of us—but he didn't falter, didn't move. Instead he wrapped his arms tight around us and held us close.

Phee*:* We were both stunned, totally unprepared for whatever this manner of attack was. Suddenly, I felt strangely warmed inside. I stopped struggling.

Adel: I saw the calm expression on Phee's face and realized that for the very first time in my life, I wasn't afraid for him or for me. Every muscle in my body gave up its tension, relaxing in the Galilean's unbreakable embrace. It may have been minutes or it may have been hours that he held us.

Phee*:* I think I might have fallen asleep, but I awoke to the commotion on the hillside. The swineherds were raving and screeching as they watched their whole herd rush down into the Sea of Galilee. They looked in our direction and saw us standing beside Jesus.

Adel: Shaking their fists at us, they ran away.

Phee: Later that day, the swineherds returned. This time they brought many people with them. Some of them were carrying sticks and torches of fire. They spoke their words and Jesus took us each by the hand and led us away, down the hill where we got into a boat and crossed the sea to his home.

Adel: That day our lives began all over again.

THE CANAANITE WOMAN (HER DAUGHTER SPEAKS)
Matthew 15:21-28

Director's Note: In this story Jesus and his disciples take time away from the turmoil brewing in Galilee and travel to Tyre and Sidon, near the great sea. A Canaanite woman, Seraphina (*serah-feena*), accosts Jesus in the street. She speaks a different language, but she knows about the man from Galilee.

It is Seraphina's daughter, Alissa, who tells the story of this foreign woman's encounter with Jesus. Alissa has heard her mother tell it many times. Brought up in a wealthy home, Alissa is a child of privilege yet a child with an impaired body. She has hyperkinesia pronounced *hyper-kin-eeseea* or *hyper-kin-eesha*. It is a neuromuscular disorder marked by involuntary, jerky movements. The cluster headaches she develops send her mother in search of the holy man.

The Canaanite Woman (Her Daughter Speaks)

My mother can be a real pain. I mean I love Seraphina, but she can be a handful when she gets pushy. She runs a very successful business as a merchant in purple goods. She is well-known and respected, and people will wait months for her custom-dyed fabrics. However, when she is on one of her missions to right a wrong, or running around recruiting supporters to chastise the city officials for shirking their duty, everyone avoids her. She goes to the city fathers on a regular basis to remind them of their responsibility to clean up the sewers, fix the dangerous potholes in the road, get the litter off the streets, and round up the overabundance of stray dogs. She takes in strays as well, but we already had three and one of them was pregnant. She warned the city that their shoddy attention to detail was bad for business. In a tourist town and major trade city, bad smells and starving dogs tend to drive the tourists away.

Seraphina isn't afraid of anyone and never hesitates to speak her mind. She's not an angry or unreasonable woman; she is passionate and persistent in her pursuits. The truth is, her arguments are usually sound and her requests fair. More often than not, she doesn't win arguments, she simply wears down her opponents. But you see, Seraphina has been on her own since she was sixteen and had to learn to stand on her own two feet.

When I was two and hadn't started to walk yet, Mom took me to see a physician who said I had weak muscles. He called my condition *hyperkinesia*. He told her there was no cure. Seraphina wasn't insulted. She just decided to take matters into her own hands. She gave what she called my "cranky nerves" a daily workout. She exercised my arms and legs for me. She kept up the routine every day. Eventually I could walk. In the beginning I would just lose my balance and fall, but I was a very determined little girl and picked myself up. When I was old enough I asked Seraphina about the jerky movements. She explained it this way: "You have cranky nerves that yell at your muscles. Every time they yell, your muscles jump because they are startled." Whenever an unpredictable sudden movement of my leg, my arm, or my face betrayed my cranky nerve condition, Seraphina simply refused to notice.

I was teased unmercifully by some of the neighborhood kids who pointed at my wide walk and ran away if my arm or leg was suddenly startled. I remember one of them asking me what was wrong with me, and just as I was about to tell her about my cranky nerves, my face suddenly curled up in a grimace. The girl screamed and ran away. Whenever the big kids tried to bully me, my mother seemed to magically appear. She would grab the ringleaders by the arm or the ear, drag them off to their own homes, and hand them off to their parents telling them, in no uncertain terms, that there had better not be a next time.

Around the time of my sixteenth birthday I began to suffer from headaches so painful that I screamed with the agony of them. They lasted for hours and days. They kept coming back, no matter what the physicians and my mother gave me to take the pain away. When the headaches came, I was beside myself. I couldn't move, or think, or even breathe for the pain.

One day Seraphina found me rocking back and forth, hitting my head against a wall. She knelt down and held my face close to hers. With tears in her eyes she said, "I don't know what horrible demon has possessed you, my darling, but he will not take you from me. Hold on, my darling girl, hold on." She left the house.

I don't know exactly when it happened, but the pain in my head suddenly disappeared. In my experience if it subsided for some minutes, I knew it would return, but it simply disappeared this time. I got on my bed and fell into a deep sleep. When my mother came home and found me sleeping, she got on my bed, gathered me close in her arms, and began to cry. In my whole life I had never seen my mother cry a single tear. I wanted to comfort her, but when I looked at her face I saw that these were not tears of sadness; they were tears of joy. She was smiling through her tears as she told me about her wild adventure chasing a Hebrew holy man through the streets of the city.

I had a million questions, but I didn't interrupt. She told me how he ignored her when she called out to him to save me from the terrible demon that was terrorizing my head. When she wouldn't relent, he stopped to speak to her and told her his work was for the sheep of the house of Israel. Seraphina is nothing if not persistent. As he turned to go, she ran ahead of him and knelt down, stopping him in his tracks. This was Seraphina's modus operandi, to dog them until they gave up or gave in. But it seemed to me out of character for Seraphina to beg anyone for anything, and particularly on her knees. "Lord help me," she said, and he still refused her, saying it was "not fair to take the children's food and throw it to the dogs."

She went on saying: "Alissa, darling, I don't know what happened. His words hurt me—yes—because I knew he was talking about me. He was talking about you and me. He described us like all those stray dogs roaming our streets. But when I answered him, the words I spoke weren't angry words. Alissa, I used his words to tell him I would accept any help he might give me. I said, 'Yes, Lord, yet even the dogs eat the crumbs that fall from their masters' table.' Just then, I saw the faintest smile on his face. I think he almost laughed. He told me I was a woman of great faith and said what I asked for would be done. That was it, and he walked away. And here you are, my dearest child, and your pain is gone!"

When we awoke the next morning, we looked at each other, tentatively, as if searching for signs of the terrible headache's return. I felt well. We dressed and set out to find the holy man whose followers called him Jesus. Seraphina insisted that we thank him. I suspected this would be a grand and public show of our appreciation, but when we found Jesus he was sitting by himself, peacefully looking out at the sea. He appeared to be about the same age as my mother. When he saw Seraphina, he stood up and the smile on his face was one of admiration. He was grinning so broadly, I could see laugh lines gathered at the corners of his eyes. He was delighted to see us.

My mother placed something in my hands and motioned me forward. As I offered him the gift, he held my hands in his. I looked down and saw for the first time the most stunning of all the purple robes my mother sold. It was a robe made for royal shoulders. Still smiling, he flung the glorious robe over his shoulders with a grand flourish and waved good-bye to us as we headed back to town.

As we walked along, I realized, perhaps for the first time, that my mother and I were the same height. I took note, too, that I was walking along beside her, not behind trying to keep up. The fluid movement of my arms and legs was a wonder to me. I lifted my skirts and jumped up a little ways, landing, to my astonishment, solidly on the ground. I could lift my leg high and kick my foot out. I wanted to run, so I did. I ran all the way back to town. It felt wonderful to be out of breath for the first time in my life. Jesus had taken not only the robe, but my cranky nerves as well.

THE CENTURION
Matthew 8:5-13; 27:54

Director's Note: The name Servius means "to preserve." The name for a private in Latin is *miles* (pronounced *meelace*). The centurion's servant is Miles. Servius serves in the Sixth Ironclad Legion of Rome and advances to regional centurion during his twenty years of service.

The background material builds the story of who Servius is when he first encounters Jesus in Matthew's Gospel. Boldface words mean emphasis is to be placed on them. It is important for the reader-actor-narrator to know he is leading the congregation all the way to the foot of the cross. Servius is, as some have put it, "Jesus' centurion." The two men meet in Capernaum in chapter 8 of Matthew's Gospel. Servius is a dignified man, a decorated soldier, who naturally stands at attention. He is not puffed up with his own importance or driven by unbridled ambition, but is a man of compassion.

See yourself standing at the foot of the cross. You are a man torn in two, a man of divided allegiance, a man changed. Allegiance to Caesar is in the centurion's job description. However, in the moment of Christ's death Servius' soul is bound to the true Son of the Divine.

The Centurion

My name is Servius. I have been a soldier in Caesar's legions for more than twenty years. When I was first recruited out of the provinces, I pledged twenty-five years of my life and loyalty to the Sixth Ironclad Legion known as "Ferrata." We served first under the great Mark Antony. Like all new recruits, I began as a private, trying not to trip over my armor. Whenever an opportunity arose I enlisted, hoping for advancement, more pay, and the benefits granted by Roman citizenship. I joined the cavalry and became a horse soldier, and later, one of the training officers with the rank of under-centurion. With each rise in rank, my pay and my wealth doubled, even tripled. I gained responsibility and staff. My deputies were hardworking and loyal, but none equaled Miles. He was assigned to me in my tenth year of service. Taking charge of my schedule, Miles organized my life, sorting out my myriad commitments so that I was able to invest appropriate time and energy in building up the cavalry, not supervising horsemen. Through his diligence, I was able to create order out of chaos and in my eighteenth year of service was promoted to the rank of district centurion, responsible for administration and law enforcement in my appointed district.

The powers-that-be sent me to the small garrison on the northern coast of the Sea of Tiberias in the town of Capernaum. Three of my deputies came with me—Miles among them. I know I was sent there to keep an eye on the Jewish population, but life was peaceful and pleasant in the fishing community. Though the fishermen exported much of their fish, those of us fortunate enough to live there regularly dined on the day's catch.

Administering the law in the region was often about settling disputes between rival business owners and keeping our eye on the slippery fingers of the local tax collectors. The cavalry made regular rounds keeping a vigilant presence in the area, and we were often resented by the people.

People had their problems, don't get me wrong, but the Jewish community was bound together by their common identity and heritage. They were well aware that they lived under the thumb of the Roman Emperor, a Gentile. They waited with certainty for their day of triumph and redemption, when God's messiah would present himself. I didn't spend much time wondering about the arrival of their messiah, having pledged my undying loyalty to Caesar, Rome's own messiah and son of god.

When the man named Jesus came from Judea and began to teach about the kingdom of his God, everything changed. For one thing, the fish my soldiers and I looked forward to eating every day were no longer in plentiful supply. Crowds of people lined the shore of the lake listening to him speak from a fishing boat, but no one was out catching fish.

He spoke to crowds everywhere, teaching in their synagogues and on hillsides, but he didn't incite his listeners; he blessed them. They listened to him for hours as he encouraged them and warned them against judging one another. People also claimed he was a healer, touching away leprosy and praying away blindness.

I busied myself with my administrative tasks until I was called away to Jerusalem to meet the new governor of Judea. I had no qualms about leaving Miles in charge of the garrison, but not long after I left he had a terrible accident. His horse was startled by a snake in the road and shied away so violently that Miles was thrown off. He landed on an outcropping of jagged rocks and when he managed to recover his breath, he found he couldn't move. The soldiers carried him back to the garrison where physicians attended to his needs as best they could, but all said there was nothing they could do. His back had been broken. When I received word of what had happened, I hurried back to Capernaum. Miles had been my right arm, my closest friend for nearly a decade. I loved him as if he were my own son.

I brought him to my home where I could supervise his care personally, but in spite of my best efforts, he was wasting away. Miles' diligent and inexhaustible spirit was ebbing away. Soon he would give up on life, and that was a loss I could not bear.

Desperate, I mounted my horse and began to ride. I had no idea where I was going or what I was riding toward or away from. Suddenly, as if appearing out of nowhere, Jesus, the holy man, was walking toward me. I reined in my horse. Could the Jewish healer help me? Would he help me, a Gentile? I didn't know how to approach him. How would he react confronted by a Roman centurion astride his horse? I dismounted and removed my helmet. Dropping my helmet and the reins to the ground, I left my horse and walked slowly toward Jesus.

He showed no alarm or distress. It was almost as if he had been waiting for me. When I came close, I lowered my gaze and told him about Miles. "Lord, my servant is lying at home paralyzed and in terrible distress." Jesus immediately offered to come to my home to help. I was stunned. This just wasn't done. Legally, Gentiles were considered unclean in Jewish circles. I was uncharacteristically tongue-tied and unable to sort out my words. Through a flood of tears I said, "Lord, I am not worthy to have you under my roof, but only speak the word and my servant will be healed." I babbled on and on. I think I gave him my credentials.

At last he said, "Go; let it be done for you according to your faith." As I turned to leave, I saw the gentle expression in his eyes as a smile came across his face. When I got back to the house, Miles was standing by his bed at attention and all I could do was fall to my knees, sobbing with relief.

I saw Jesus many times after that. I became a kind of referral service, sending all sorts of different people to see him and listen to his teachings.

When I was transferred three years later to take charge of Pontius Pilate's Praetorian Guard, I hated to leave Capernaum. I left the people in good hands. Miles was their new district centurion.

In Jerusalem, I found crucifixions were not rare. It was the accepted method of capital punishment for insurrectionists, zealots, and anyone who threatened the integrity of Caesar's empire. But when Jesus was brought before Pilate to stand trial, I wanted to hide my face in shame.

Our eyes met, and it was as if I could read every one of his thoughts: relief—perhaps at recognizing a friend—fear, and determination. For the first time I was ashamed to be a Roman soldier, but if I walked away—if I hid myself away—there would be no one with him. I know it sounds ironic, maybe even cruel, but I stayed with him. I walked alongside him every step of that long and arduous way. I was there when he faltered and fell. I heard his every cry and every word he spoke, as we drove the nails into his hands. On his face, even through the pain, was that ever-forgiving and tender expression. At the sound of his final cry, I felt the earth shaking beneath my feet and I heard myself say: "Truly this man is God's Son!"

The Worship Service

ON THE MARGINS
A GOOD FRIDAY SERVICE

PRELUDE

*CALL TO WORSHIP (From Psalm 69)
   All: Save me, O God. Do not let those who hope in you be put to shame because of me. Answer me, O Lord, for your steadfast love is good; according to your abundant mercy, turn to me. Do not hide your face from your servant, for I am in distress—make haste to answer me.

*OPENING HYMN "What Wondrous Love Is This" Hymnal #292 (verse 1)

AFFIRMATION OF FAITH
   We believe in God the creator of heaven and earth, the giver of light and truth, life and breath. We believe that nothing can separate us from the grace, love, and mercy of God who never hesitates to forgive the repentant heart.
   We believe in Jesus Christ, God in human vesture, who desired to be in this life with us, reaching out to love us into new life. We believe that he took upon himself our sin and regret carrying these to the cross, where he gave himself unto eternity for our sakes. This was his ultimate gift to us.
   We believe that his death was not the end and that he will come again one day.
   We believe in the Holy Spirit, who speaks a fiery, passionate truth to all people, in every language. Our hearts are warmed and we become the living proof of God's transforming presence.
   We believe that we are the church, the body of Christ, called to serve and to make a difference in God's world.

THE LORD'S PRAYER
   Our Abba, Father, in heaven, holy, holy, holy is your name. May your kingdom come, and your will be done on earth as it most surely is in heaven. Give us this day the food we need and forgive us our sins as we forgive the sins of our neighbor. Guide us in right paths. Lead us away from temptation and keep us from evil; for yours is the kingdom and the power and the glory forever. Amen.

HYMN OF CONTRITION "Ah, Holy Jesus"   Hymnal #289 (verses 1-3)

SCRIPTURE READING Matthew 27:11-23

THE GADARENE DEMONIACS

SCRIPTURE READING Matthew 27:24-31

HYMN OF CONTRITION "Ah, Holy Jesus" Hymnal #289 (verses 4-5)

SCRIPTURE READING Matthew 27:32-44

THE CANAANITE WOMAN

OFFERTORY THOUGHT

Matthew tells a unique story of Judas Iscariot publicly repenting of his betrayal of Jesus. Unfortunately, he reports his regrets and his desire to give back the money he was paid for his betrayal to those who have no interest. In an effort to wash his hands of it all, he throws the thirty pieces of silver clattering onto the stone floor of the temple. Matthew tells us that the chief priests took the "blood money" and purchased the potter's field, the place where clay was extracted from the ground for making pots. Not useful for farming or agriculture, it became a common grave for those people who existed on the margins of Judaism who could not be buried in an orthodox cemetery. Those who are marginalized by our society have much to teach us. Our goal as Christians must be to include them in our life.

OFFERTORY

*DOXOLOGY "What Wondrous Love Is This" Hymnal #292 (verse 2)

*UNISON OFFERTORY PRAYER

Gracious God, we offer these gifts with humble hearts. Bless them, we pray, to do your work and will in the name of the Christ. Amen.

PREPARATION HYMN "O How He Loves You and Me" TFWS #2108

SCRIPTURE Matthew 27:45-50

THE CENTURION

CLOSING HYMN "Beneath the Cross of Jesus" Hymnal #297

(During the singing of this hymn, the single Christ candle that has been burning on the altar is removed from the sanctuary as the lights dim. Then the strepitus sounds, and slowly and solemnly the Christ candle is returned to the altar.)

*BENEDICTION

Go in peace to love and serve as never before.

POSTLUDE "Were You There" Solo

As you leave the sanctuary during the postlude, please observe the solemnity of this occasion by departing in silence.

(*) Please stand as you are able.
Hymnal is *The United Methodist Hymnal,* and **TFWS** is *The Faith We Sing.*

Out of Darkness

NARRATIVES BASED ON THE GOSPEL OF MARK

Characters for Readings
- Peter's Mother-in-Law, Mark 1:29-31
- The Leper, Mark 1:40-45
- The Man Forgiven (Nahum's Daughter Speaks), Mark 2:1-12
- Levi, the Son of Alphaeus, Mark 2:13-17

Intended Message of These Stories
All of these stories reveal God's intention for us in the life, ministry, and death of Jesus. The Mark stories reveal how our lives can be changed and are changed as we open ourselves to the care of Jesus.

PETER'S MOTHER-IN-LAW
Mark 1:29-31

Director's Note: Peter's mother-in-law is a woman of substance who worked diligently and consistently to make a life for her daughters and herself. She is not a whiner or a victim; neither is she an exhausted survivor or a martyr. She is truly a woman who understands that there is much to be said for being able to work. She loves having her home full of fishermen, feeding them while she listens to the stories they tell. Don't play her as depressed or downtrodden. She is a woman of unconquerable spirit; that is what Jesus saw in her.

Peter's Mother-in-law

Yes, I knew Jesus. We lived in the same town—Capernaum—it means *Village of Comfort*. I am a widow. It happened a long time ago, when my husband's fishing boat sank in a sudden storm on the Sea of Galilee. I was devastated and so frightened, with two little girls and no other family to help me out. I wondered how we would survive. I knew I couldn't let any grass grow under my feet, so I started cooking meals for the fishermen and tradesmen at the port. We made a modest living and managed to hold on to the house my husband built, even though I was forced to sell much of the equipment he had purchased to run his fishing business. We had to in order to keep our heads above water.

With so few assets and me approaching my middle years, I was not likely to marry again. However, my daughters, Rivkah and Hannah, would marry when they came of age. Rivkah married first. She married a man named Peter, a young fisherman just starting out. Peter and his brother Andrew had fishing in their blood, but they had limited resources and were struggling to get a foothold in the trade. We gave them everything we had left of my husband's equipment: some casting nets and a trammel net with weights, sinkers, and cork floats in good repair, a sail, oars, and a fishing boat in need of repair. The two brothers came to live with us in my home, and we became a family business.

My daughters and I worked, separating the catfish and the eels from the clean fish with scales. We dried, counted, and salted the fish, packing them in baskets for export to Rome and Jerusalem. My son-in-law's skill as a fisherman grew and his good reputation served him well. Zebedee—the biggest fisherman in town—took note of his skilled competitors and invited Peter and Andrew to partner with him and his sons, James and John.

Life, at last, was comfortable and enjoyable. My kitchen was always full of fishermen telling their stories of mighty storms and great catches. It did my heart good to see them well fed and contented. Remembering the lean years, I was happy to host dinners, serving my best meals to friends, visitors, and business partners. There was always room for a few more at our table.

In the spring of the thirty-fifth year of the reign of Herod Antipas, while helping to dry the nets, I got my arm caught on a stray fish hook and ripped open a sizable wound. I soon came down with a fever and collapsed in the kitchen. I don't remember much. What I do remember is that I was unable to move, eat, or talk. My daughters were terrified, but I knew the merits of my son-in-law, and whatever happened to me, Rivkah and Hannah would be safe.

I was fully aware that I was dying when, quite suddenly, I felt a hand on mine. It was a man's hand. I saw his face, his intense eyes looking into mine, but I was unable to say anything to him, to explain my condition or warn him. He took my hand in his and then as he lifted my arm, I found myself offering him my other hand. He pulled me gently into a sitting position. Before I knew it I was standing and walking with him around the room. I gave a little jump just to test my strength and found myself giggling like a child taking her first steps. The young man chuckled as I jumped again and began to dance around the room.

Quite without shame I ran to him and embraced him. "Who are you and what is this that you have done for me?" He embraced me back, saying: "God is good, always," and left my room to join Peter, Andrew, James, and John in my sadly neglected kitchen. I washed and dressed and as I came into the kitchen was greeted with applause, more embraces, and joyful tears. It was then I was introduced to the man who saved my life—Jesus. Indeed I am triumphant, a woman so very grateful to be alive again, able to do what gives me the greatest pleasure: offering friends and strangers comfort—helping **them** weather life's storms. I know storms will come; they may be mild or they may wreak havoc, but eventually they will pass. That is the time when we need help to sort through the devastation left in its wake. On a day when I believed I would take my last breath, the grace of God entered my room and redemption found his way into my heart. My life goes on and I have only Jesus to thank.

THE LEPER
Mark 1:40-45

Director's Note: This is a gentle story, and the character of the leper is revealed as a young man just getting started in his life. There needs to be urgency in his voice as he tells about the day the rug was pulled out from under him. Yes, he tried to stay rational, trying not to panic as he jumped through all of the hoops required by the priests as they determined his fate. If he has leprosy it will mean the end. He can't be with his family, his wife, or his children. We tend not to think about or envision the terrible grief that envelops someone with a disease that has no cure. Numerous hearts are broken in this story, not just one. (If you need to get a taste of what it is to be forgotten, take a walk through a nursing home.) Lepers were taken from their loved ones and isolated from society. This man is ashamed, mortified, and powerless, giving up everything to go and live among the other lepers. What he discovers is a community. This young man's leprosy may have been healed by Jesus, but his heart and soul were nurtured and healed in the community of lepers. We do not live in isolation.

The Leper

Yes, I met Jesus. I was married with two young children when I noticed the dark patchy spot on my arm. I covered the spot, thinking it was a bug bite of some sort; I believed it would eventually disappear. But when a similar scaly patch appeared on my face, I couldn't hide it and knew there was something terribly wrong. I went to the priests; I made sacrifices—wondering what sin I had committed or what sin my ancestors had committed that I should be so stricken with sores.

I spent two weeks with the priests, where they observed me and gave me treatments for my skin. This had to be done because it was the priests who would make the ultimate decision regarding my fate. They were not unkind when they told me I had leprosy. But they said there was nothing to be done. I had to leave the village. I had to leave my family, so they wouldn't become infected. I told no one but my wife and let everyone else believe that I had simply disappeared one day.

The priests took me to a place several miles outside of town where there was a colony of people like me and dropped me off. The leader of the colony—Jeremiah—greeted me. I think I was in a state of shock, unable to think or speak or even see clearly. This just couldn't be happening.

I don't know what let it loose—fear, rage, or absolute grief, but I heard an anguished cry escape from the center of my soul and echo in an endless scream—then everything went black. I awoke in the morning, swaddled in blankets on a mattress of straw, and was offered bread and a cup of honeyed wine—the best I had ever tasted. Mortified, I arose, still a bit shaky, and Jeremiah led me out into the fresh morning air.

What I saw next was amazing; these lepers were hard at work, tending to a small vineyard and a field of wheat. They grew their own food, made their own wine, and dried their own fruits. They were trying their best to sustain themselves, and that made me feel even more ashamed of my display the evening before. After a few days, I was working in the vineyard. Eventually I took on the job of welcoming and caring for any newcomers brought to the colony. My wife, who is an incredibly brave woman, came to see me every week in the wee hours before dawn. Through her tears, she shared the stories of our children's adventures and assured me that they were all right.

When she suddenly stopped coming, I didn't know what to think. Maybe she was ill. Desperate to know, I left the colony in the middle of the night, walking toward town. In the dark I got lost and couldn't find my direction. I would have to wait until daylight to find my way back to the colony. As I sat cold and shivering, waiting for the sun to rise, I heard footsteps and saw a figure moving toward me. He stopped and sat down on the ground, and I heard him talking to himself. No, he wasn't talking to himself, he was singing. It was a familiar psalm. The tune and the words were soothing and familiar; I could feel a calm coming over me as I joined him in prayer. We prayed together throughout the night. In the morning when the sun peeked out from behind the hills, I recognized him. He was the rabbi who was teaching in the synagogue the day I first went to the priests. People said he was a healer, someone who cast out unclean spirits. Who was more unclean than I? I turned to him and fell to my knees: "If you choose, you can make me clean." He looked at me with sorrowful eyes and stretched out his hand to touch me. I flinched—uncertain. If he touched me, wouldn't he be made unclean and possibly catch the disease? As his hand touched me, he spoke. His voice was powerful and strong, "I do choose. Be made clean!" And I was clean. The patches of bad skin were gone and I felt alive again from the inside out.

He told me not to tell anyone, but I ran into the village to my home and couldn't wait to tell my wife. She hadn't been ill; instead she had been giving birth and caring for our new son. We named him *Jesus,* after the man who had given us life again. You may ask what I do now—I have traveled to all of the neighboring towns to tell my story to everyone who would listen. I work as a fisherman with Zebedee on one of his boats, with a crew of three others. It's a good job and he is a generous boss. Each week he gives me a full basket of fish to take to Jeremiah and the people I call my other family on the outskirts of town. They, in turn, give some of their best honeyed wine for Zebedee and me.

THE MAN FORGIVEN (NAHUM'S DAUGHTER SPEAKS)
Mark 2:1-12

Director's Note: Just about everyone who has ever attended church knows the story of the man who was lowered through the ceiling of a house to be healed by Jesus. He is the man forgiven. It is his daughter who will give us insight into the man who so needed to be forgiven. His name is Nahum. Since her mother's death, the daughter has become the matriarch of the family. She is always positive with a hopeful outlook on life. She knows her family well and seeks to be the reconciling presence in the house. She is always working to build up the family, offering her own creative perspective. She is mature, probably beyond her years. She is savvy, but not flippant or uncaring.

The Man Forgiven (Nahum's Daughter Speaks)

My father was a stonemason carving mortars and pestles, mill wheels to grind flour, and olive presses from the plentiful lava rock around

Capernaum. He had four sons, all of whom he hoped would be stonemasons. He dreamed of the day when he would place the sign over the door that read: *Nahum and Sons Stoneworks*. We were five children devoted to our parents. Our dad worked very hard from dawn until well after dusk building his business, keeping the vision of the day he would welcome his sons as his partners. When he was fourteen, my oldest brother, Benjamin, took me aside and confided, "I don't want to be a stonemason. I want to go to sea and sail ships." When I asked him where on earth he had gotten that notion, he answered, "King Solomon's navy; they were talking about it in our history class." Astonished by his grandiose plan, I said, "But Dad is expecting all of you boys to work with him." Ben just rolled his eyes and nodded. When he announced his dream of becoming a sailor to my father, the response was "Over my dead body!" and that was the end of the discussion.

Josh was the next eldest boy. Naturally strong and muscular, he eventually grew taller than Ben. As a little boy he loved going to the stoneworks with my dad. He always came home banged up with bruises and scrapes. We dismissed his lumps and bumps because he was a boy who loved to climb and jump around on stuff. He was bound to fall now and then.

One day my father's apprentice, Isaiah, came running toward my father carrying Josh in his arms, blood streaming from Josh's head. When my father asked what happened, Isaiah told him, "I was watching him climb around on the rocks. He was having a great time when suddenly he stiffened and fell to the ground. I ran over to him and found him—his eyes were rolled back—his arms and legs were stiff, with the muscles stiff and rigid all over. He hit his head when he fell. I have never seen anything like it. I thought he was dying. When his body relaxed, he was still breathing, so I ran over here to you. But Nahum, he won't wake up."

My father took Josh to a local physician who said Josh had epilepsy. There was no treatment or cure except to have the unclean spirit inside him removed. My father's response to that prescription was never to let Josh near the stoneworks or the physician again.

Ben tried once more to reason with my father about his desire to be an adventurer on the high seas, but Dad cut him off and Ben left home without another word. I know my father was brokenhearted, but he never spoke Ben's name again. He began spending more time at the stoneworks than at home. He stayed out very late, returning home only after the family had gone to bed. He was often drunk, bumping into the furniture and cursing the pain. As the years passed, my two youngest brothers, Abel and Nahum Jr., had only a distant, but always respectful, relationship with my father. It was as if he had lost interest in bringing his sons into the business.

As it happened, Isaiah and I were to be married. He had become my father's right hand. Hardworking, trustworthy, and handsome, he had become my father's right hand. We met on one of those nights when he was kind enough to bring my father home when Dad drowned his disappointments in too much wine. Unbeknownst to my father, Isaiah spent time with Josh, Abel, and Nahum Jr., teaching them everything he knew about stonemasonry.

One dreary spring morning my father woke up and couldn't move. He could speak and move his head, but his legs and his arms seemed to be tied to the bed. The look in his eyes was one of terror. I had never seen my father so vulnerable, so afraid. Days turned into weeks with no change. He gave instructions to Isaiah on managing the business and, in turn, Isaiah relied on Josh, Abel, and Nahum to help him keep the stoneworks running.

Despair crept into my father's eyes, as if his spirit were being drowned in a sea of regret. Josh came home from the synagogue one day, talking about a man with the power to heal people. His name was Jesus, and Josh had seen someone healed that very day. Josh convinced us to bring my father to this wondrous healer to see if there was anything he could do for him. We searched for Jesus, but couldn't find him. At the synagogue someone told us he had gone away. Just when we were about to give up hope that Dad could be made well, we learned that Jesus had returned to Capernaum. That evening Isaiah, Josh, Abel, and Nahum Jr. came to Dad's room carrying a board with a straw mat lashed to it. They lifted the man, whom I had seen as unbreakable and indestructible through all my growing-up years, onto the board, and carried him to a house across town.

There were crowds of people lined up outside the door and when we saw them we almost gave up. Then Josh suddenly climbed up onto the roof shouting, "Okay, everybody, lend a hand and help us lift my father up onto the roof." Isaiah and my other brothers joined Josh, and the four men hauled my father—board and all—up onto the roof. Isaiah and Josh used pickaxes to cut a hole in the roof's thick thatching. There was great commotion, inside the house and outside, over the destruction of the roof, causing the crowds to back away from the door enough for me to slip into a spot at the entrance where I watched as my brothers and my husband lowered my father through the hole in the roof. It was quite a spectacle to watch as they managed not to drop him, but set him gently down on the ground in front of Jesus.

I saw Jesus look up at the four faces peering through the destroyed roof. I watched as their worried expressions disappeared, giving way to expressions of calm, relief, and absolute trust. Jesus' eyes lingered for a moment on Josh, and he smiled as if he recognized my brother. Then he turned his gaze on my father and said, "Son, your sins are forgiven." My father looked with a strained expression into the face of Jesus. His eyes were full of questions. Jesus, not much older than my brother Ben, was calling my father "son." Some of the scribes in the room seemed put off by Jesus' words as well.

I confess none of us had any idea what to expect; we figured that Jesus, as a man known to heal people, would, at the very least, place a hand on my father. But he didn't. Suddenly, I saw my father's face change. His eyes were bright and alive; he was smiling. A visible peace came over him and his whole body appeared to let go of some terrible weight. It was as if I saw him give up his disappointments, his regrets, and all of his unfulfilled expectations. I watched my father's life restored as Jesus said to him, "Stand up, take your mat and go home." Miraculously, my dad stood up, picked up the mat, and, as natural as you please, he waved to my brothers and my husband to come down off the roof. On the way home we all walked past the stoneworks to show Dad the new sign hanging over the door. It read: *"Nahum and Sons Stoneworks."*

LEVI, THE SON OF ALPHAEUS
Mark 2:13-17

Director's Note: The *P* in Ptolemies is not pronounced. The word is pronounced *Tall-eh-mees*. Seleucids is pronounced *Seh-loosids*. "The Caesars" is correct, since every Roman emperor after Julius Caesar was called Caesar. The true character of Levi is revealed as the story evolves. He is pretty matter-of-fact at the outset. There is almost a pompous air about him as he speaks, but his message is self-deprecating. This narrative intends to educate a bit because most folks have no clue about the Romans' system of taxation and merely write off tax collectors as evil. Gentiles and Jews were taxed on everything, including their heads. It is probably true that many of the tax collectors were unscrupulous and on a par with gangsters. But knowing that makes Levi's sudden and mysterious conversion even more riveting. The suddenness of his decision is a testament to the power of Jesus. Levi is, in a moment, completely and totally disarmed by Jesus. Like the fishermen, Levi drops everything to become a devoted follower of Jesus. As he stands in the shadow of the crucifixion, wondering what will happen now, he vows to carry on because for him, there *is* no turning back.

Levi, the Son of Alphaeus

No matter what anyone tells you and no matter how many times you ask, you never really understand *why* a person does a thing. The "why" of anything can be understood only by the person who does it! Why the master called me to follow him is still a mystery to me. Why I decided to follow him is yet another mystery. Believe me when I tell you that I am not keeping some intricate secret; it's just that I can't give you a rational explanation for what I did. There are those who look down their righteous noses at those of us who collect Caesar's taxes. Quite frankly, I think we are preferable to the alternative, which would likely be a fully armored legion of Roman soldiers.

All right, maybe that's an exaggeration. Maybe the emperor wouldn't send a legion of soldiers—more than five thousand—but he would send plenty.

As members of the tribe, so to speak, the tax collectors see themselves—some would say falsely—as keepers of the peace. As long as we were the ones collecting money for Caesar, the soldiers wouldn't have to and our people would be relatively safe. To our way of thinking, it was that simple. Taxes were and are as inevitable as death, and the Caesars exacted them from us as did the Ptolemies and the Seleucids before them. Collecting taxes was a service provided for the local and the state government. Our work required fastidious record keeping and a full understanding of various kinds of taxes: the ground tax on property and, of course, the income tax, import and export duties, and taxes levied on all that was publicly sold and bought. Farmers paid one-third to one-half of their taxes in produce, whether grain, livestock, fruit, or wine; the remainder they paid in coin. Merchants always paid in coin. Local taxes were required to maintain public buildings, such as the synagogue, and to keep the roads and city walls in good repair. The crown tax was required to support the Roman Emperor and **our** king, too. On top of the civil tax, one had to pay the religious tax; the coffers for both could be found side by side in the Temple in Jerusalem.

My father and I made a good living. We did not live lavishly in comparison to some of the more unscrupulous publicans, but we were quite comfortable. I think the most difficult part of our work was dealing with those who could not pay their taxes. Interest accrued on unpaid taxes, but we were willing to work out payment plans to assist those who found it easier to pay their taxes in smaller amounts more frequently. If taxes went unpaid, the consequences were severe, including imprisonment and the loss of one's home, property, and often one's family members, who might be sold into slavery. This occurred more often than I care to remember.

Our A & L tax office—that's Alphaeus and Levi—was on the caravan route connecting Damascus with the Mediterranean. We were situated perfectly at a major point of entry into Palestine from the north and the east.

The day I met the rabbi Jesus it didn't take me long to figure out who he was, since he traveled with a small entourage followed by a big crowd.

Everyone was talking about him—you hear a lot in a tax office. I remember one day a fellow looking me straight in the eye saying, "That Jesus can make diseases disappear; I wonder if he could do the same to you." We were immune to such barbs and sarcasm. We knew people said much worse things about us behind our backs.

All foot traffic and wheeled vehicles were required to stop at the tax office and pay the "head" tax, or merchant tax, whether they were planning to stay in town or were just passing through. The day Jesus came to the office, I didn't even look up from my ledger, but held out my hand to receive his tax, to be recorded on the page. I knew someone was standing there, but his hands were resting on the counter, palms down. Since he made no move to retrieve a coin from his purse, I looked up and I saw, for the first time in many years, a face that was smiling—he looked genuinely glad to see me. We had never met, but he looked at me as if he had known me all my life. His face gleamed and I was speechless. I am never speechless, but I was so disarmed by his presence and his demeanor that I just stood there—awestruck.

After a long and puzzling silence, he reached out his hand and said, "Levi, follow me." I did! I can't tell you why. But I have followed him since that day. I have followed him all the way. I have never looked back on what I left behind, what might have been, or what could have been had I not followed. Why did he choose me? I was one of the most hated men in Capernaum and the most likely to be scorned. Nevertheless, he called and I answered.

In the end I am left wondering what it was all for—he's been taken from us and murdered by those who were afraid of him. I have no answers; I can only say that tonight my sorrow is greater than any I have ever known. In this moment, I am more afraid as one who followed Jesus than I ever was being a tax collector for Caesar. But there is no turning back for me now.

The Worship Service

OUT OF DARKNESS
A GOOD FRIDAY SERVICE

PRELUDE

CALL TO WORSHIP (From Psalm 28)

LEADER: To you, O LORD, I call; my rock, do not refuse to hear me, for if you are silent to me, I shall be like those who go down to the Pit. Hear the voice of my supplication, as I cry to you for help.…I lift up my hands toward your most holy sanctuary.

PEOPLE: Blessed be the LORD, for he has heard the sound of my pleadings. The LORD is my strength and shield; in him my heart trusts; so I am helped and my heart exults, and with my song I give thanks to him.

ALL: The LORD is the strength of his people…the saving refuge of his anointed. O save your people, and bless your heritage; be their shepherd, and carry them forever.

SCRIPTURE READING Mark 14:53-65

*OPENING HYMN "What Wondrous Love Is This"   Hymnal #292

CONGREGATIONAL PRAYER

Wondrous God, giver of life and granter of grace, we come before you this evening humbled by the weight of Jesus' burden. This day, more than any other, confounds us. We cannot comprehend the sacrifice made on our behalf. We have known many men and women throughout history who have given their lives for causes of justice, for human rights, for loyalty to country, and for love. Your willingness to take our sins—not make them magically disappear, but to take them upon yourself—is too astounding, and we scarcely can take it in. What could possibly have been your purpose in bearing the sins of human-kind, past and present? Was it to release us from the burden of our regrets, our shame, our sorrow, our grief? Was it to release us from every weight that fetters us to the world? Did you carry these on your person to the cross to make room in our hearts for the kingdom of God? Open our eyes to see that these burdens have been taken from us and have been nailed to the cross with YOU. Bless the Lord, O my soul. Amen.

PETER'S MOTHER-IN-LAW

SCRIPTURE READING Mark 14:66-72

HYMN OF CONFESSION "Ah, Holy Jesus"   Hymnal #289

THE LEPER

SCRIPTURE READING Mark 15:1-15

THE MAN FORGIVEN (NAHUM'S DAUGHTER SPEAKS)

SCRIPTURE READING Mark 15:16-32

OFFERTORY THOUGHT

Sacrifice: "a giving up of something valuable or important for somebody or something else considered to be of more value or importance." This is the first definition of the word *sacrifice* in the Encarta Dictionary. I guess maybe John was right when he wrote about God valuing—more than himself—the *kosmos,* that is, the universe, the arrangement of the stars, the heavenly hosts, right down to the whole mass of human beings, even those who don't know God (John 1).

OFFERTORY

*DOXOLOGY "O How He Loves You and Me" TFWS # 2108

UNISON PRAYER

Gracious God, on this night of nights when Jesus gave himself for us, making the ultimate sacrifice, we offer not only our gifts, but ourselves to love and serve your creation. Bless this offering to your service. In the name of the Christ we pray. Amen.

LEVI, THE SON OF ALPHAEUS

SCRIPTURE READING Mark 15:33-40

HYMN OF MOURNING "O Sacred Head, Now Wounded" Hymnal #286

SCRIPTURE READING Mark 15:42-47

*CLOSING HYMN "Must Jesus Bear the Cross Alone" Hymnal #424

*BENEDICTION

Now, go out into the world remembering the eternal grace of God, the love of Jesus Christ and ever-presence of the Holy Spirit. Love and serve them with all of your heart, soul, mind, and strength. Amen.

POSTLUDE "Were You There" Solo

As you leave the sanctuary during the postlude, please observe the solemnity of this occasion by departing in silence.

(*) *Please stand as you are able.*
Hymnal is *The United Methodist Hymnal,* and **TFWS** is *The Faith We Sing.*

YEAR C
There Is a Balm

NARRATIVES BASED ON THE GOSPEL OF LUKE

Characters for Readings

- The Samaritan, Luke 10:25-37
- Woman with the Alabaster Flask—Myra, Luke 7:36-50
- Joanna, the Wife of Chuza, Luke 8:1-3; 23:50-56; 24:1-10

Intended Message of These Stories

Balms, spices, and scented oils appear in the Hebrew Scriptures and Christian Scriptures. They are used for healing and anointing, symbols, and gifts. In Matthew's Gospel the magi bring gifts to the newborn king. The frankincense and myrrh are gifts as precious as gold. They perfume the air with their aromatic qualities and heal wounds with their medicinal properties. In these three stories gleaned from the Gospel of Luke, the Balm of Jericho is used to heal a broken Jesus, to anoint Jesus the ever-empowering friend, and to remind us that he is ever-present in our walk through life.

THE SAMARITAN'S STORY
Luke 10:25-37

Director's Note: The story of the Samaritan is itself a story unique to Luke. What follows is a different kind of interpretation of the man left for dead on the Jericho road: the man left for dead is Jesus himself. The names of the characters are Greek words transliterated into pronounceable English. Axel Playsohn is "Good Neighbor" and Pandock Hues is the "Innkeeper."

The Samaritan's Story

I am a maker and trader of fragrant oils, ointments, and balms. My family and I work to extract the gummy resin of the balsam trees that grow in my hometown of Jericho. It takes months for the buds of the tree to be cured into the aromatic oils, balms, ointments, and expensive perfumes we sell, but I promise you the waiting is worth it. The fragrance is captivating and freshens any room in the house. The ointments and balms have incredible healing properties. They soothe and cool inflamed areas and will keep a wound from getting infected. Some have told me that our Balm of Jericho actually soothes the pain of the wound as it heals. Rubbed into muscles, tired and sore from long hours of work, the balm helps ease the discomfort. Listen to me; I am going on and on as if I were trying to sell you the product.

I have a story to tell you. We have many clients in Jericho, but our products are also very popular in Jerusalem among Jews and Gentiles alike. There are many Jews who have no qualms about trading with a Samaritan, especially if the product is as good as ours. The Romans can't tell us apart. I guess, in their minds, we all look alike. Neither do they care to understand the cause of the rift between Samaritans and Jews. It doesn't make sense to me, either, that people who worship the same God and are descended from the same Abraham will not work to settle the argument over where the Temple should have been built after the Exile. Enough of that. Back to the story.

I travel over the mountain to Jerusalem all the time to deliver our balm to clients. Our eclectic clientele is always growing and includes soldiers, Roman dignitaries, rich women—Jewish and Gentile—courtesans, priests, and physicians. Rarely do they begrudge me the considerable cost of the product because it can be used in so many ways. At certain times of the year, when Samaritan, Jewish, and Gentile holidays coincide, it is difficult for us to keep up with the demand.

My family and I make a good living, and I like my work. I particularly like hearing about all the different ways my clients find the ointments and oils useful. Not that my clients invite me in for tea to tell me all about it; they report on its efficacy as they pay me and quickly close the door. My physician clients use it liberally on patients injured in all manner of accidents or battles. I know how very well this balm works to heal, having used it on a man I found half dead on the Jericho Road.

I had finished making my deliveries in the city and wanted to make it home by sundown, when the Sabbath would begin. It is usually faster coming down the eleven miles than it is going up. The road is very rocky and rough, running alongside the deep chasm that is part of the wilderness that is the Judean desert. It was about three o'clock in the afternoon, and the sun was setting in the sky. I had only a short time to get home before the Sabbath began. The Jericho road is not one to be traveling after dark, either accompanied or alone. I came upon what looked like a dead body at the side of the road. The two people I had passed minutes earlier heading up to Jerusalem had offered no warning, but being Jewish holy men, they were not obliged. I crossed the road to take a closer look and I heard him moan. He wasn't dead, but was most certainly on the brink. Besides being beaten up, he looked half-starved as if he hadn't eaten in weeks. Naked and bruised from head to foot with dried blood on his face, his torso, and in his hair. His nose was broken and his lips torn. His eyes were swollen shut. His own mother wouldn't have recognized him. He looked more like a corpse than a living, breathing man, but he was alive. I had to help him. My efforts might not save him, but I couldn't just leave him as he most certainly would die.

I brought some wine for him to drink, and moistened cloths with it to cleanse his wounds. Then I applied my healing balm to his wounds and wrapped them with clean cloths. I removed my own cloak and wrapped him in it. I offered him more sips of wine as we rested together in the shadows. I asked him who had done this to him, assuming he had been attacked by bandits. He could barely speak through his swollen lips and parched throat, and was probably delirious. I can't be sure, but it sounded like he said, "The devil." Then he passed out. He needed care, rest, food, and water. He needed a physician, but first he needed to be rescued from this deadly place and brought to safety.

I lifted him up and placed him on my donkey. Together we made our way down the mountain. He was still out of his head most of the way, and I fought to keep him astride the animal. When we finally got to town, I brought the stranger to the Jericho Inn where the innkeeper, Pandock Hues, is a friend of mine. He was a bit skittish about having a half-dead Jewish stranger as a guest in his inn. Jews don't stay the night in a Samaritan city unless they have to. Pandock wanted no repercussions if the man died in his establishment. I paid Pandock the cost of the room and board for a few nights plus a bit more, asking him to send out for some clothes and sandals for the man's feet. I promised to return and pay the whole bill, no matter how many days the stranger needed to recuperate and get back on his feet. Together we carried our patient to the nicest room in the inn. Once more, we cleaned his wounds and applied the healing balm to his cuts and bruises. I left the balm for him to use as he needed, and opened a bottle of perfumed oil to give the room a pleasant fragrance. I patted the stranger's hand as I was leaving, promising to return. Suddenly the stranger, quite in his right mind, reached out and clasped my hand in his. He held on tight, mustering all of the strength he could. Forcing his eyes open, he looked at me, his expression full of questions and tenderness. A tear fell from his eye as he said, "I will never forget your kindness to me. What is your name?" "My name is Axel," I said. "Axel Playsohn, and what is yours?" "My name is Jesus." That was all he said as his hands let go of mine, and he dropped back onto the pillow and fell sound asleep. "May God's blessings be upon you, Jesus, and may you be healed and strong when we meet again."

I returned the morning after the Sabbath to see how he was getting on, but he was gone. Pandock reported that his guest ate and slept through the night on Friday and all day Saturday. But the next morning when he went to bring him breakfast, both the stranger and the balm were gone. I settled the bill with Pandock and went on my way.

That was three years ago. I never saw the Jewish stranger again, but then I probably wouldn't recognize him without a swollen face. Perhaps he would remember me.

Today I am headed up to Jerusalem to make holiday deliveries. I am bringing two animals loaded down with product. With so many pilgrims in town for the Passover holiday, I am sure to find new buyers for my Balm of Jericho.

THE WOMAN WITH THE ALABASTER FLASK—MYRA
Luke 7:36-50

Director's Note: Myra is a graceful woman. She is a sweet person and should not be played as a hardened, cynical urchin of the streets. She is a lady now and, as far as we are concerned, always has been, whether taking money for her favors or bringing up her sons and managing her vineyard. When she proclaims herself a widow by day and a harlot by night, it is said matter-of-factly, not with discomfort in her voice. Neither is it said with amusement or with a raised eyebrow. The only occasion for the raised eyebrow and a voice of experience is when she says: "Myra **knew** Simon." It is a telling statement that she **knew** Simon as a woman who had shared her favors with him on numerous occasions. She is not breathy or whimsical. She is not a siren. She is a woman who refused to be a victim of circumstances or society. She is not made to feel ashamed by her encounter with Jesus, but further empowered by her friendship with him.

The Woman with the Alabaster Flask—Myra

I have not always had to do this work to survive and feed my children. I was married at sixteen to a man chosen for me by my parents. He was a good man, and we were a good match. He owned a vineyard just outside the city of Emmaus. He took meticulous care of the vines, and those who worked for him thought him a fair boss. I worked alongside him, learning how to care for the vines, pruning them, determining when they were ready for the harvest. We had two sons. His parents were no longer alive. My parents lived in the city proper and cared little about farming.

When I was just twenty-six, my husband fell ill and died. My sons were still very young, too young to work in the vineyard. My husband had no siblings—no younger brothers to take on the duty of husband. The workers were not eager to follow my lead as the manager of the vineyard. The death expenses took what little we had saved over the years. We just didn't have the money to hire an experienced manager. I had to figure out a way to save our home and our vineyard, which are my husband's legacy.

I went into the city to ask my parents for a loan, but they confessed they had no confidence in my ability to carry on in my husband's stead. It was too risky, and if I failed it would cost them dearly. My father was brutishly insensitive, telling me to find an old man to marry and get on with my life. I was still mourning my husband, and left their house in a rage.

Feeling dejected, defeated, and helpless, I wandered the streets of the city and soon found myself in an area totally unfamiliar to me. As it grew dark, I became frightened, realizing I was utterly lost. I began to run back the way I thought I had come, and as I rounded a corner, I crashed into a woman, nearly knocking her down. She grabbed me by my shawl—I thought to catch herself, but she glared into my face and raised her arm to slap me, but she stopped quite suddenly and said, "Who are you? And what are you doing walking the streets of 'the district'?"

"I'm afraid I don't know what you mean by 'the district,'" I said. "I am so sorry I bumped into you, but I am quite lost. I was just trying to find my way home."

"Dearie, you found your way into the district, and it's much too late for you to be walking these streets alone. Tell you what, you look like a nice enough young lady. You can stay the night at my place; I have plenty of room. You can go home in the morning. Let's get you something to drink to warm you up."

"Maybe I had better go back to my parents' house."

"You could do that too," she said. "But first let's have a sip of wine to calm your nerves."

That was the night I made friends with Cleo, a woman of the district, that is, a woman of the streets. Cleo, that very night, showed me how to survive as a woman, not a helpless widow.

No doubt about it, the work was demeaning as well as demanding, but it was what I chose to do to feed my family and keep a small portion of the vineyard productive.

I lived as two different women, the vineyard owner and a woman of the night. By day I was a widow, by night I was a harlot. I lived that lie for five years, with no one being the wiser. I was known to my clients as "Myra," famed for the lovely scented perfumes and oils I used in my work. They were mixed especially for me by Axel the Samaritan. He sold balms and ointments that smelled like heaven. I bathed in them and the aroma served as a magnet, summoning all those willing to pay for my favor.

One evening I was walking to my corner of the district when a man stopped short and looked at me, somewhat confused. He smiled at me like a long lost friend.

I was a bit taken aback. He didn't look like a potential customer. He didn't leer at me, or coo, or make suggestive remarks; he just asked the name of the perfume I was wearing. I answered that it was a special preparation called the Balm of Jericho. He brightened even more and said: "I would recognize that fragrance anywhere. The man who makes that balm saved my life."

At that statement, I was so intrigued, I invited him to tell me his story. He introduced himself as Jesus from Nazareth. We talked about everything, and I told him my story. He held me in rapt attention until the wee hours of the morning. Every story he told me about all the people he had met in his travels lifted my spirits. He had actually seen the blind regain their sight, the insane return to their right mind, and the dead brought back to life. He had even known lepers who were cured.

Everything about this man was extraordinary, except his appearance. His clothes and his face were ordinary, but his eyes had an intensity unlike any others. In his presence something inside me was changing. My spirit felt refreshed—my imagination was filled with new ideas, new thoughts, and new possibilities.

When it was time for me to head home to the vineyard, his words lingered in my thoughts. They felt like a fire burning within me. I shouted to the heavens as I walked: "I will be the master of my own vineyard; I will take back my life, and no longer will I be a woman of the district!"

It was an extraordinary moment. It was an extraordinary decision. Today, Myra would leave the district behind forever. There was just one more thing I had to do.

That evening I returned to the city in search of the man who saved my life, and brought with me the most expensive jar I owned of the balm. It wasn't difficult to find him. After an incident in the local synagogue, his name was known all over town. Tonight he was dining with Simon the Pharisee.

Myra knew Simon. I found his house, walked in, and walked over to Jesus. Simon was apoplectic, but he said nothing.

When I saw Jesus, something inside me broke wide open. I fell at his feet, sobbing. What were these tears? Tears of grief, of sorrow, of relief, of joy—perhaps all of these—fell upon his skin. I rubbed the salty drops into his feet with my hair—as if cleansing them with every bit of the sadness and sorrow that flowed from my heart. I then broke open the jar of expensive Balm of Jericho and poured that over his feet. As I did so, Jesus spoke to the other guests. I didn't hear what he was saying until he took my head in his hands and looked into my eyes. In a strangely commanding voice, he said, "Your sins are forgiven." We stared into each other's eyes for a moment. Then I dried my tears and stood up. I stood tall, looked at each guest, and walked out into my future as I heard Jesus' final farewell, "Your faith has saved you; go in peace."

JOANNA, THE WIFE OF CHUZA
Luke 8:1-3; 23:50-56; 24:1-10

Director's Note: Joanna is mentioned by name in chapter 8 of Luke's Gospel as a woman of means. In other words, it was her credit card that was being swiped to cover the cost of food, clothing, and lodging on the road from Galilee to Jerusalem. She is not a woman of leisure, although she lives in a palace. She is the wife of a high-ranking member of Herod's personal staff.

Do not play her as arrogant or haughty. She doesn't like the trappings of the palace. She doesn't like Herod. She found Jesus in her search for purpose and meaning in her life. She has a courageous heart, but isn't fully aware of it. As she tells her story, her account of events of the Passover becomes more urgent, distressed in its telling. Don't talk faster, but be obviously more moved, more impassioned as you relive the events in your mind's eye. There should be a sense of relief in your voice as you recite the last lines of the story. The *Ch* in the name of Joanna's husband, Chuza, is pronounced as it is Chanukah (*Hanukkah*); it is a guttural—*Hoozah.*

Joanna, the Wife of Chuza

My name is Joanna, and I have been a follower of Jesus for a good portion of his ministry. It's not information I share with many people, since my husband is Herod's personal steward. As the ruler of the Northern Region, Herod built a city complete with a stadium and a splendid palace on the Sea of Galilee. He named the city Tiberius in honor of the Roman emperor who appointed him. My husband, Chuza, and I reside in Herod's palace, which is Greek in style and very ornate, with figures carved on the outer walls.

My curiosity about Jesus began soon after Herod—in one of his more petulant moods—executed John the Baptist. Soon afterward there were rumors circulating that a man named Jesus from Nazareth was John the Baptist come back from the dead.

My days living in the palace were not heavy with chores. I often went out for long walks to get away from the toxic environment of the palace, with its daily dramas and feuds among the relations.

One day as I walked along the shore of the Sea of Galilee, I saw a man speaking to a crowd of people. He was actually standing in a boat a short distance from the shore. He talked about God in a way I had never heard before. I was captivated by his simple and uncomplicated invitation to everyone who had ears to hear. I realized that this was the man from Nazareth I had heard rumors about. I worried for a brief second that I might be pointed out as a member of Herod's household, maybe even a spy. No, that would never be the case; I didn't look the part. More often than not, I was taken for one of the hired help rather than the wife of a high-ranking servant. Nevertheless, I kept quiet about my interest in Jesus and what I did on my frequent outings.

Herod's concern over Jesus' growing popularity turned into an obsession. People said that Jesus was Elijah, others said that he was a prophet, and some whispered that he was the Messiah. Herod sent out spies and listeners to find out everything Jesus was doing and saying.

Jesus had close followers, both men and women. There were some fishermen who had left their businesses, their families, their hearth and home to follow him. Although I sought out every opportunity to hear him speak, I kept my distance and a low profile, but I saw how he transformed people's lives. He seemed willing to be in anyone's company, rich or poor, saint or sinner, clean or unclean.

I wanted for nothing and lived very comfortably within the palace walls, but my heart and mind were inextricably drawn to Jesus and his life-changing work. I wanted to serve **him**, not Herod. *How could I become part of this ministry?* I wondered. If I was gone for more than a few days, my husband would become concerned, and the last thing he needed was more worry.

I made a plan. I told my husband that I was planning a trip to visit my parents in Jerusalem for a few weeks. He was so busy with tending to Herod's constant demands that he left the arrangements for my journey to me, assuming I would be safely escorted to my destination.

It may have been ill-advised and impulsive, but I left the palace unescorted and joined the entourage following Jesus. Crowds followed him to open fields and deserted places and camped out, refusing to leave or go home. Indeed, he was a man of miraculous deeds, and on one occasion he managed to turn five loaves of bread and two fish into a meal that satisfied thousands. And the disciples even collected a basket of leftovers.

One evening, when we stopped for the night, I mustered my courage to approach those who were in Jesus' inner circle. As I came close, I heard a few of the disciples saying they needed to get food. Since I had purchased food along the way, I had bread, fruit, and dried fish to share. It could be for all of us. Somewhat clumsily I spoke up to offer what I had, and was greeted by Jesus inviting me to join the group. Everyone was grateful, but the truth was, I had means and was eager to help.

The two women disciples—Mary and Susanna—embraced me as a sister. They had been healed by Jesus, and shared their very personal and moving stories with me. Susanna was widowed, left destitute by her husband's family, and Mary had been brutalized by her drunken father. They were strong women, devoted and smart. I was honored to be with them. From that evening on, my days were full of meaning and purpose. As one of Jesus' disciples, I found that my unremarkable life now held promise. Mary, Susanna, and I ministered to Jesus and the rest. We were joined by Jesus' own mother, the mother of James and John, the two sisters Mary and Martha, and more. Those of us with means supported our brothers and sisters.

I returned to put in an appearance at the palace from time to time. My poor husband was so busy trying to manage Herod's paranoia and his mania for building things, that he seemed relieved to think of me going off to enjoy myself elsewhere.

Looking back, one can see that the signs were clear that a change was coming. Rumors abounded that Herod wanted to rid Galilee of Jesus. Jesus decided to leave Galilee and go to Jerusalem, to be in the city for the Passover holiday. He had to have known that Herod also journeyed to Jerusalem for the same reason.

Everything that happened in Jerusalem happened so quickly and unpredictably that it seems more like a blur than reality. From the moment we arrived, Jesus seemed to be doing everything he could to stir up resentment against him. He was not one to keep a low profile. The day Peter, James, and John returned, the men came from the Temple telling how Jesus, in a fury, had enraged the priests by overturning the tables of the money changers. Suddenly, everything was thrown off kilter. The very air we breathed seemed weighed down with gloom. We were all very nervous as we made the preparations for the Passover feast and sensed that something was terribly wrong. And we were right.

Jesus was arrested that very night, dragged off by thugs. Peter told us how he watched Jesus being tried for blasphemy before the twenty-three judges on the Sanhedrin. The verdict was guilty. Because Jerusalem was under Roman jurisdiction, the council was obliged to bring Jesus before the Roman governor, Pontius Pilate.

We had no idea what was going on until word came to us that Jesus was being marched out of the city to be crucified—a punishment reserved for those guilty of capital crimes. Stricken with grief and nearly paralyzed with fear, we stood at a distance and watched as the guilty were punished on the hill called The Skull. We were helpless to save the life of our Lord, our leader, our master, who had blessed us so and instilled in us a passion for living.

When it was all over, Mary, Susanna, and I went with Joseph from Arimathea, who had claimed Jesus' body, to a tomb newly hewn out of rock. Joseph wrapped Jesus' body in a fresh linen shroud, and laid him in the tomb to keep him safe until the twenty-four hours of the Sabbath had passed. It fell to my sisters and me to make ready the spices and oils to anoint his body two days hence. Not having anticipated the task, we were unprepared.

We held on tight to each other as we crept out of the tomb leaving the dear one behind. We saw a stranger approaching and began to move off in the other direction, but he called after us. He spoke with a tremor in his voice saying: "Pardon me, are you the women who are followers of the man called Jesus who was crucified?"

We stopped, afraid to turn around, not knowing if he meant to accuse us or comfort us.

"We spent a little time together, three years ago," the man said. "I am most grieved to hear of his death. Please let me give you something. I know you must prepare his body for burial." His eyes filled with tears as he said, "I realize you may be hesitant to take a gift from a Samaritan, but it would be a kindness to me, and I believe this balm will help you in your task." He held out a jar of his ointment, and I recognized the sweet, soothing fragrance immediately; we all did. Jesus carried a jar of this same balm with him. He used it to soothe his road-weary feet. I clutched the jar to my heart and thanked Jesus' Samaritan friend as he went on his way. As we walked on, surrounded by the fragrance of the balm, it felt as though Jesus walked with us.

The Worship Service

THERE IS A BALM
A GOOD FRIDAY SERVICE

PRELUDE

*CALL TO WORSHIP

    All: Save me, O God. Do not let those who hope in you be put to shame because of me. Answer me, O Lord, for your steadfast love is good; according to your abundant mercy, turn to me. Do not hide your face from your servant, for I am in distress—make haste to answer me.

*OPENING HYMN "In the Cross of Christ I Glory"   Hymnal #295

AFFIRMATION OF FAITH

    We believe in God the creator of heaven and earth, the giver of light and truth, life and breath. We believe that nothing can separate us from the grace, love, and mercy of God who never hesitates to forgive the repentant heart.

    We believe in Jesus Christ, God in human vesture, who desired to be in this life with us, reaching out to love us into new life. We believe that he took upon himself our sin and regret, carrying these to the cross, where he gave himself unto eternity for our sakes. This was his ultimate gift to us. We believe that his death was not the end, and that he will come again one day.

    We believe in the Holy Spirit, who speaks a fiery, passionate truth to all people, in every language. Our hearts are warmed and we become the living proof of God's transforming presence. We believe that we are the church, the body of Christ, called to serve and to make a difference in God's world.

THE LORD'S PRAYER

    Our Abba, Father, in heaven, holy, holy, holy is your name. May your kingdom come, and your will be done on earth as it most surely is in heaven. Give us this day the food we need and forgive us our sins as we forgive the sins of our neighbor. Guide us in right paths. Lead us away from temptation and keep us from evil; for yours is the kingdom and the power and the glory forever. Amen.

HYMN OF CONTRITION "Ah, Holy Jesus"   Hymnal #289 (verses 1-3)

SCRIPTURE READING Luke 23:26-38

THE SAMARITAN'S STORY

SCRIPTURE READING Luke 23:39-43

HYMN OF CONTRITION "Ah, Holy Jesus"   Hymnal #289 (verses 4-5)

SCRIPTURE READING Luke 23:44-49

THE WOMAN WITH THE ALABASTER FLASK—MYRA

OFFERTORY THOUGHT

Luke describes individuals *casting lots* after Jesus says, "Father, forgive them, for they do not know what they are doing." Casting lots was a method used to foretell the future or determine something by chance. In Old Testament stories, priests threw painted dice or bones onto the ground—cast lots—to determine which goat was to be sacrificed to the Lord and which goat would serve as the "scapegoat," carrying upon its back all of the sins of the children of Israel. The scapegoat was sent off into the wilderness alone. So as the soldiers cast lots near the cross, Jesus took on both roles of the Old Testament: as the sacrifice and as the one who carried our sins upon his back.

OFFERTORY

*DOXOLOGY "Praise, My Soul, the King of Heaven" Hymnal #66

*UNISON OFFERTORY PRAYER

Gracious God, we offer these gifts with humble hearts. Bless them, we pray, to do your work and will in the name of the Christ. Amen.

PREPARATION HYMN "O Love Divine, What Hast Thou Done"

Hymnal #287 (verses 1-2)

SCRIPTURE Luke 23:50-56

JOANNA, THE WIFE OF CHUZA

CLOSING HYMN "O Sacred Head, Now Wounded" Hymnal #286
(During the singing of this hymn, the single Christ candle that has been burning on the altar is removed from the sanctuary as the lights dim. Then the strepitus sounds, and slowly and solemnly the Christ candle is returned to the altar.)

*BENEDICTION

Go in peace to love and serve as never before.

POSTLUDE "Were You There" Solo
As you leave the sanctuary during the postlude, please observe the solemnity of this occasion by departing in silence.

(*) Please stand as you are able.
Hymnal is *The United Methodist Hymnal*, and **TFWS** is *The Faith We Sing*.

CPSIA information can be obtained
at www.ICGtesting.com
Printed in the USA
JSHW020400060421
13299JS00005B/79